TAX STRATEGIES FOR THE ONE-PERSON BUSINESS
(2013-2014 Edition)

Written by
Christopher J. Inglese, CPA, MS (Tax)

DISCLAIMER

This publication is designed to provide accurate and authoritative information in regard to the subject matter covered. It is sold with the understanding that the publisher is not engaged in rendering legal, accounting, or other professional service. If legal advice or other expert assistance is required, the services of a competent professional person should be sought.

Copyright © 2013 by Small Business Publishing, LLC

TABLE OF CONTENTS

Copyright © 2013 by Small Business Publishing, LLC

OVERVIEW

Whether your business is organized as a corporation, a limited liability company, or a sole proprietorship, you (and/or your one-person business) are probably paying much more tax than is required by law, and don't even know it. Delegating all tax planning to your accountant, believing that he or she is providing you with the tax-saving advice you need, may be a mistake.

Most accountants, who accept one-person businesses as clients, typically do not possess advanced tax education and/or in-depth experience. Many are too busy filling-in forms to provide innovative tax-saving advice to such small clients. Those who do in fact possess a Masters Degree in Taxation and have decades of professional experience, spend most of their time getting new business for their firm and managing their staff. It is the low-level staff person who is assigned to the one-person business, while knowledgeable and experienced tax accountants focus their tax planning skills on large corporations and wealthier individuals.

This booklet is intended to explain, in plain English, the most valuable and widely applicable tax-saving strategies available to the one-person business. It is up to you to familiarize yourself with these strategies, and then consult with your present tax advisor to determine if they

Copyright © 2013 by Small Business Publishing, LLC

are appropriate in your particular situation. You are ultimately responsible for the taxes you pay.

The majority of one-person businesses unfortunately pay thousands of dollars in unnecessary taxes each year. Don't be one of them.

Copyright © 2013 by Small Business Publishing, LLC

LEGAL FORMS OF A ONE-PERSON BUSINESS

A one-person business can operate under one of three different legal forms:

- Sole Proprietorship
- Limited Liability Company
- Corporation

A limited liability company (LLC) with one owner, which does not elect to be treated as a corporation, is treated as a sole proprietor for tax purposes. A corporation or LLC can elect to be taxed as an S corporation, or in the absence of an S election, could be considered either a personal service corporation or a regular corporation. The legal form of the business therefore does not necessarily control these four different tax treatments available to the one-person business:

- SOLE PROPRIETORSHIP or DISREGARDED LLC ENTITY

Absent an election to be treated as a corporation, a one-person limited liability company is generally disregarded as an entity and is therefore treated as a sole proprietorship for tax purposes. Income from such businesses is reported each calendar year on Schedule C of the owner's individual income tax Form 1040 and is

Copyright © 2013 by Small Business Publishing, LLC

taxed at the owner's personal tax rates. All of the business income is considered "earned" by the owner, and is subject to self-employment tax (also known as FICA, which is comprised of Social Security tax and Medicare tax). The owner is required to remit taxes via estimated tax payments each "tax quarter".

- S CORPORATION

A corporation or LLC, which makes an "Election by a Small Business Corporation" using IRS Form 2553, is generally not considered a tax-paying entity. Net income from the S corporation (after deducting the shareholder-employee's salary and bonus) is reported each calendar (or fiscal) year on Schedule E of the shareholder-employee's individual income tax Form 1040 and is subject to only income tax at the owner's personal tax rates. (There generally is no tax at the time the S corporation distributes income already reported, or to be reported, on Schedule E.)

Salary and/or bonus payments to the shareholder-employee are the only amounts considered "earned" by him/her and therefore only these amounts are subject to FICA taxes (as well as income tax). The shareholder-employee's FICA and income taxes are withheld from his/her salary and bonus. (Estimated tax payments might also be required to cover taxes on income reported on Schedule E.)

Copyright © 2013 by Small Business Publishing, LLC

- PERSONAL SERVICE CORPORATION
A one-person corporation, or an LLC which has elected to be taxed as such, which is engaged in one of the professions (health, law, engineering, architecture, accounting, actuarial science, the performing arts, or consulting) is considered a personal service corporation. Net income from such a corporation (after deducting the shareholder-employee's salary and bonus) is taxable to the corporation at the flat federal tax rate of 35 percent. This same income (not paid out to the shareholder-employee as salary or bonus) is generally taxed again when distributed to the shareholder. (For this reason, most, if not all, of a personal service corporation's income is typically paid out each year as salary and bonus to the shareholder-employee.) The salary and bonus is considered "earned" by the shareholder-employee and therefore subject to FICA taxes (as well as income tax). The shareholder-employee's FICA and income taxes are withheld from his/her salary and bonus.

- REGULAR CORPORATION
Net income (after deducting the shareholder-employee's salary and bonus) from a corporation, or an LLC which has elected to be taxed as such, which is neither an S corporation nor a personal service corporation, is taxable to the corporation at graduated federal tax rates (15% on first $50,000, 25% on the next $25,000, 34% on the next $25,000, 39% on the next $235,000, etc). This same

Copyright © 2013 by Small Business Publishing, LLC

income (that is not paid out to the shareholder-employee as salary or bonus) is generally taxed again when distributed to the shareholder. For this reason, all but $50,000 of corporate income is typically paid out each year as salary and bonus to the shareholder-employee, to take advantage of the lowest corporate tax rate. The salary and bonus is considered "earned" by the shareholder-employee and therefore subject to FICA taxes (as well as income tax). The shareholder-employee's FICA and income taxes are withheld from his/her salary and bonus. (Corporate estimated tax payments might also be required to cover taxes on the income that is taxable to the corporation.)

Copyright © 2013 by Small Business Publishing, LLC

SAVING SELF-EMPLOYMENT TAX (FICA)

GENERAL TAX STRATEGY

Self-employment tax (also known as FICA tax) is comprised of Social Security tax and Medicare tax. It is generally imposed only on a taxpayer's "earned income". The typical American taxpayer pays more in self-employment tax and/or FICA tax than he/she does in income tax. The general tax strategy is to clearly separate "earned income" from "unearned income", so that the self-employment tax (or FICA tax) is imposed only on income earned from the labor or services provided by the taxpayer. Even though saving the Social Security portion of the FICA tax now, may result in a reduction in future government benefits later, it is generally believed that the taxes saved can be better invested by the taxpayer to yield a much greater future retirement benefit.

SOLE PROPRIETORSHIP OR DISREGARDED LLC ENTITY

Since all income reported on Schedule C of Form 1040 is subject to self-employment tax, there is little a sole proprietor (or owner of a disregarded limited liability company) can do to save self-employment tax. However, he or she can hire his/her children under the age of

Copyright © 2013 by Small Business Publishing, LLC

eighteen. The "reasonable" wages paid to such children are not subject to FICA tax, but still reduce the parent-owner's self-employment tax. (See next section entitled SHIFTING INCOME TO LOW BRACKET FAMILY MEMBERS regarding additional potential income tax savings.) Also, self-employment tax can be saved by properly allocating portions of deductible expenses to Schedule C (ex/ business portion of income tax preparation fee, portion of car loan interest and property tax relating to its business use, etc).

S CORPORATION

Since only the shareholder-employee's salary and bonus are subject to payroll tax, S corporations provide an opportunity to separate "earned income" from "unearned income", thereby saving a significant amount of FICA tax. By reducing the shareholder-employee's salary and bonus ("earned income") to a low but "reasonable" level, only that amount of income will be subject to FICA tax. The remaining non-salary income, not subject to FICA tax, can be withdrawn tax-free as a distribution of profits.

It is unclear what comprises a "reasonable" level of salary and bonus. Court cases and IRS rulings have confirmed that $ 0 is not "reasonable" compensation. Some of the factors to consider when determining a shareholder-employee's "reasonable" salary and bonus are:

Copyright © 2013 by Small Business Publishing, LLC

- the time spent working by the shareholder-employee
- the type of work being performed by the shareholder-employee
- the salaries of non-shareholder-employees doing similar work
- the portion of profits derived from labor of non-shareholder-employees
- the portion of profits derived from capital invested in the corporation

The Social Security portion of the FICA tax rate is 12.40% of wages up to $113,700 (in 2013), while the Medicare portion of the FICA tax rate is 2.90% of all wages. There is however an additional .90% employee Medicare tax on wages in excess of $125,000 (if Married Filing Separate), $200,000 (if Single) or $250,000 (if Married Filing Joint). The 12.40% and 2.90% rates are paid 50/50 by the employer and the employee, with the employer's half deductible for income tax purposes. Since a shareholder in a one-person business is both the employer and the employee, the actual FICA tax rate for someone in the 28.00% income tax bracket would be about 13.16% on the first $113,700 (in 2013). If a shareholder-employee were to reduce his salary and bonus from $85,000 to $60,000, about $3,290 in after-tax FICA could be saved every tax year. However, if the shareholder-employee has wages from outside the S corporation and these wages, when combined with S corporation wages, exceed the annual $113,700 Social Security wage base, higher Social Security tax would

Copyright © 2013 by Small Business Publishing, LLC

probably be incurred as a result of incorporation (or electing to be taxed as a corporation).

If an unmarried sole proprietor, with $200,000 of Schedule C income, were to incorporate and set his/her salary at $115,000, approximately $2,120 of Medicare tax could be saved every tax year (after taking into account a 28% employer income tax deduction). The savings could even be higher if such sole proprietor's Schedule C income is in excess of $200,000 (by avoiding the additional .90% Medicare tax).

It is important to note that a 3.80% Medicare tax is also imposed on "unearned income" for taxpayers with Adjusted Gross Incomes in excess of $125,000 (if Married Filing Separate), $200,000 (if Single) or $250,000 (if Married Filing Joint). The profit from an S corporation, that flows through to shareholders who "materially participate" in the business, is not considered "unearned income". This Medicare tax will therefore generally not be imposed on net income from one-person S corporations.

PERSONAL SERVICE CORPORATION

A personal service corporation's net income (after deducting the shareholder-employee's salary and bonus) is taxable to the corporation at the flat rate of 35 percent. Whatever income is left, after the payment of this

Copyright © 2013 by Small Business Publishing, LLC

corporate-level tax, is generally taxed again to the shareholder when distributed. Because this double taxation includes a high corporate tax rate, it is typically beneficial to zero-out the income taxable to the corporation by maximizing the shareholder-employee's salary and bonus before each year-end. However, by paying out all income to the shareholder-employee in this way, all of the business income becomes subject to FICA tax. As a result, the shareholder-employee of a personal service corporation can do little to reduce FICA tax.

REGULAR CORPORATION

A regular corporation's net income (after deducting the shareholder-employee's salary and bonus) is taxable to the corporation at graduated tax rates (which rise to 34% or more on corporate net income in excess of $75,000), then it is typically taxed again to the shareholder when distributed. Because the corporate tax rate on the first $50,000 of corporate net income is taxed at only 15%, it is typically beneficial to adjust the shareholder-employee's salary and bonus each year so that corporate net income does not exceed this threshold amount. The goal is to ensure that the net income left in the corporation is taxed at a marginal income tax rate that is lower than the shareholder-employee's marginal income tax rate. In addition to this income tax savings, limiting the salary and bonus paid to the shareholder-employee also avoids FICA tax. There is also no FICA tax when

Copyright © 2013 by Small Business Publishing, LLC

the net income, which was left in the corporation, is eventually distributed to the shareholder as a dividend. (See later section entitled TAKING ADVANTAGE OF LOW TAX RATES ON CORPORATE INCOME AND ON DIVIDENDS for a more detailed discussion of this topic.)

Copyright © 2013 by Small Business Publishing, LLC

SHIFTING INCOME
TO LOW BRACKET RELATIVES

GENERAL TAX STRATEGY

Each individual taxpayer pays income tax based on a graduated tax rate schedule, with marginal federal income tax rates ranging from 0% to 39.60%. Individuals with higher income therefore pay tax at higher marginal rates. The general tax strategy is to save income tax by "shifting" income from taxpayers subject to the higher tax rates (ex/ 39.60%), to taxpayers subject to the lower rates (ex/ 0%). Of course, no one wants to "shift" their income to an unrelated person just to avoid tax. (No one wants to give up $1.00 to save only $.396.) However, one might consider saving tax by "shifting" income to a low tax bracket relative who will benefit from that income anyway, such as a dependent child or parent.

SOLE PROPRIETORSHIP OR DISREGARDED LLC ENTITY

Since all income of a sole proprietorship, or disregarded limited liability company, is reported on Schedule C of Form 1040, such a taxpayer can "shift" income by hiring his/her relative (typically a child or parent). As long as a "reasonable" salary or wage is paid to the relative, the taxpayer can save tax by deducting it as a business

Copyright © 2013 by Small Business Publishing, LLC

expense. The low tax bracket relative, reporting the salary or wage as income on his/her own individual tax return, pays little or no income tax.

The taxpayer should be able to prove "reasonableness", by having the relative keep timesheets detailing the work he/she does each day. Since salary or wage income is considered "earned income", it is not subject to the tax rule which taxes "unearned income" of children under the age of 19 (and some full-time students age 19 to 23) at their parent's marginal tax rates. See above section entitled SAVING SELF-EMPLOYMENT TAX (aka FICA) regarding additional potential self-employment tax savings of hiring children under the age of eighteen.

S CORPORATION

Since income from an S corporation is reported each year on the individual income tax returns of its shareholders, based on their percentage of stock ownership, S corporations provide a unique opportunity to "shift" income by issuing stock to low tax bracket relatives. A child or parent, owning 25% of the S corporation's stock, will report 25% of the income from the S corporation on his/her personal tax return. In order for this tax strategy to work, it is important that the child or parent be the "true" owner of the stock, not just the "legal" owner. He or she must behave as a shareholder and exercise his/her power as such. It is also important that "reasonable"

Copyright © 2013 by Small Business Publishing, LLC

wages be paid to all shareholder-employees for services actually performed. Lastly, shareholder children must be at least 24 years of age (18 if not a student or if child's earned income exceeds his/her support), if corporate income is to be taxed at their low individual tax rates, rather than the parent's higher rates.

Unlike a sole proprietorship or disregarded limited liability company, FICA tax is incurred if an S corporation pays salaries or wages to children of shareholder-employees under the age of eighteen. However, since there is no FICA tax on S corporation profits (after deducting the shareholder-employees' "reasonable" salaries and bonuses), there is a FICA tax advantage to shifting income via the issuance of S corporation stock (rather than via the payment of salaries and wages) to low tax bracket relatives.

PERSONAL SERVICE CORPORATION

Like a sole proprietorship, or disregarded limited liability company, a personal service corporation usually "shifts" income only by employing its shareholder-employee's relative (typically a child or parent) at a "reasonable" salary or wage. This is the case since it is beneficial to zero-out the income taxable to a personal service corporation, primarily through the use of salaries and bonuses, before each year-end.

Copyright © 2013 by Small Business Publishing, LLC

REGULAR CORPORATION

Net income retained in a regular corporation (after deducting salaries and wages of its shareholder-employees) is taxed first at the corporate level, then again at the shareholder level when that income is distributed as dividends. Because dividends must be paid in proportion to stock ownership, and low tax bracket relatives typically are minority shareholders, it is generally better to "shift" income via the payment of salaries and wages, rather than the issuance of regular corporate stock. However, issuing stock to low tax bracket relatives, and paying dividends to them, may make sense where all of the shareholder-employees are in low tax rate brackets (15% or less on salary and wage income, and 0% on dividend income).

When determining the amount of salaries and wages to be paid to relatives, the overriding goal is to ensure that salaries and wages are "reasonable", and that the net income left in the corporation is taxed at a marginal income tax rate that is lower than that of the shareholder-employee. (See later section entitled TAKING ADVANTAGE OF LOW TAX RATES ON CORPORATE INCOME AND ON DIVIDENDS for a more detailed discussion of this topic.)

Copyright © 2013 by Small Business Publishing, LLC

DEFERRING TAX BY CONTRIBUTING UP TO 100% OF YOUR EARNED INCOME TO A RETIREMENT PLAN

GENERAL TAX STRATEGY

Like a Traditional IRA, money contributed to a retirement plan is deductible and its earnings grow tax-deferred. Income tax is incurred only when the original contribution and its earnings are distributed, typically when the individual taxpayer is retired (and usually in a low tax bracket). The tax deduction for the contribution allows the taxpayer to earn income on money that otherwise would have been paid in income tax. The tax-deferred earnings compound each year, allowing the money to grow faster (without the imposition of income tax). The general tax strategy is therefore to maximize contributions to retirement plans (to the extent allowed by law).

There are many types of retirement plans available to the one-person business (such as the SEP, the SIMPLE-IRA, the 401(k) Profit Sharing Plan, and the Defined Benefit Plan). This booklet will focus on only the 401(k) Profit Sharing Plan which, other than perhaps the Defined

Copyright © 2013 by Small Business Publishing, LLC

Benefit Plan, allows the maximum contribution for the one-person business. A SIMPLE-IRA (which is similar to the 401(k) Profit Sharing Plan) should be considered by the smaller one-person business with limited funds.

The amount that can be contributed to a 401(k) Profit Sharing Plan is comprised of an employee contribution plus an employer contribution. The maximum employee contribution for the 2013 tax year is $17,500 ($23,000 for an employee age 50 and older). In 2013, the maximum employer contribution is 25% of up to $255,000 of "earned income". The total of these amounts cannot exceed an overall maximum amount of $51,000 in 2013 ($55,500 if age 50 and older). The 401(k) Profit Sharing Plan (as well as the SIMPLE-IRA) allows up to 100% of "earned income" to be contributed to the retirement plan. In 2013, a one-person business, with earned income of $23,333, can contribute all $23,333 to the retirement plan (25% of $23,333, plus $17,500 from the employee-owner assuming he/she is less than 50 years of age).

The 401(k) Profit Sharing Plan is fairly flexible. The employee need not make a contribution. The employer typically must make "substantial and recurring" contributions, though not every year. (For "safe harbor" plans, the employer contributions may have to equal 3% of "earned income".) The Plan need not cover part-time employees (those working under 1,000 hours a year), nor employees under age 21 (ex/ children of the owner). The

Copyright © 2013 by Small Business Publishing, LLC

401(k) Profit Sharing Plan should be in existence for at least 5 to 7 years, or the life of the business (whichever is shorter).

As long as the owner and/or his/her spouse are the only employees, there is very little administration. When retirement plan balances total $250,000, a fairly simple 5500EZ form must then be filed (within 7 months of year-end). It is important to note that if employees (other than the owner's spouse or children under age 21) are hired, the costs of administering a 401(k) Profit Sharing Plan could be approximately $1,000 per year. In this case, a SIMPLE-IRA should be considered, in lieu of the 401(k) Profit Sharing Plan, to avoid the administration costs.

SOLE PROPRIETORSHIP OR DISREGARDED LLC ENTITY

All income reported by a sole proprietorship or disregarded limited liability company is considered "earned" income. As a result, this type of one-person business, with a "safe harbor" 401(k) Profit Sharing Plan, would be required to make an employer contribution equal to 3% of the Schedule C income (adjusted for the contribution itself, as well as the deduction for one-half of the self-employment tax). As a result of this complex calculation, the owner has little control over the amount of the minimum required contribution each year. Also,

Copyright © 2013 by Small Business Publishing, LLC

since a sole proprietorship or disregarded limited liability company pays more self-employment tax than other types of one-person businesses, the maximum allowable Profit Sharing contribution is lower (because of the adjustment for one-half of this additional self-employment tax).

S CORPORATION

Since only the shareholder-employee's salary and bonus is considered "earned income", an S corporation with a "safe harbor" 401(k) Profit Sharing Plan, would be required to make an employer contribution equal to 3% of only that salary and bonus. As a result, by adjusting his salary and bonus each year, the shareholder-employee has a great deal of control over the amount of the annual minimum contribution required each year.

In order to reach a combined employee and employer contribution of $51,000 (2013 maximum), a shareholder-employee under the age of 50 must have a salary and bonus totaling only $134,000 ($51,000 equals the employer contribution of 25% of $134,000, plus the $17,500 employee contribution). Sole proprietorships or disregarded limited liability companies, must have higher "earned income" in order to reach the same $51,000 maximum. In addition, the owner of these other non-corporate entities may pay extra self-employment tax on earnings in excess of the amount needed to reach the

Copyright © 2013 by Small Business Publishing, LLC

maximum 401(k) contribution. The S corporation thus may allow its shareholder-employee to pay himself/herself just the right amount of salary and bonus, to maximize the 401(k) Profit Sharing contributions while minimizing the FICA taxes.

PERSONAL SERVICE CORPORATION

It is typically beneficial to zero-out the income taxable to a personal service corporation through the use of salaries and bonuses (as well as related FICA tax and retirement plan contribution deductions) before each year-end. As a result, this type of corporation has little control over the amount of its 3% minimum required 401(k) "safe harbor" contribution each year. Also, the personal service corporation and its shareholder-employee might pay extra FICA taxes on salaries, in excess of the amount needed to reach the maximum 401(k) contribution.

REGULAR CORPORATION

The overriding goal in a regular corporation is to ensure that the net income left in the corporation (after the deductions for salaries, bonuses, employer FICA tax, and retirement plan contributions) is taxed at a marginal income tax rate that is lower than that of the shareholder-employee. Tax deductions for employer FICA tax expense and employer retirement plan contributions, must be considered in reaching this goal.

Copyright © 2013 by Small Business Publishing, LLC

DEDUCTING MEDICAL EXPENSES WITHOUT LIMITS

GENERAL TAX STRATEGY

Medical expenses of an individual, and his/her dependents, are generally deductible on Schedule A of Form 1040, but only to the extent they are in excess of 10% of his/her Adjusted Gross Income (7 ½ % if the taxpayer or spouse is age 65 or older). For this reason, most individuals get little or no income tax deduction for medical expenses. The general tax strategy is therefore to have the one-person business pay the medical expenses and deduct them as a business expense (a fringe benefit to its employee).

SOLE PROPRIETORSHIP OR DISREGARDED LLC ENTITY

A sole proprietorship, or disregarded limited liability company, generally may not deduct medical expenses of its owner and his/her family, even if the business has set up a Medical Reimbursement Plan for all of its employees. Such a plan may reimburse medical expenses for the non-owner employees, their spouses and their dependents. The owner deducts such reimbursements as a business expense (as a fringe benefit to the employees). Such a deduction saves the owner both income tax and

Copyright © 2013 by Small Business Publishing, LLC

self-employment tax, while the non-owner employees do not have to report the medical expense reimbursement as income.

There is however, a "tax loophole" available to the sole proprietorship or disregarded limited liability company, when the owner's spouse and/or child is a legitimate employee of the business. In this case, the business may reimburse and deduct medical expenses for that employee-spouse or employee-child, as well as for his/her own spouse and dependents. Interestingly, medical expenses of the owner are thus reimbursable and deductible, when the owner is the spouse of the covered employee-spouse.

The Medical Reimbursement Plan must be written and established before the reimbursable medical expenses are incurred. Also, since it may not discriminate between employees, any non-relative employees must also be eligible to participate.

S CORPORATION

There is no income tax deduction allowed for most fringe benefits (example/ Medical Reimbursement Plan), provided by S corporations to shareholders who own greater than 2% of its stock. Fringe benefits provided to family members of such shareholders are also not deductible, regardless if those family members are

Copyright © 2013 by Small Business Publishing, LLC

employees of the S corporation. The shareholder-employee must report any such medical expense reimbursement received as W-2 income.

PERSONAL SERVICE CORPORATION

A shareholder-employee of a personal service corporation may participate in a Medical Reimbursement Plan without having to report the expense reimbursement as personal income. The corporation deducts the medical expense reimbursement as a business expense (a fringe benefit to the shareholder-employee), without limitation. The Medical Reimbursement Plan must be written and established before the reimbursable medical expenses are incurred. Also, since it may not discriminate between employees, any non-relative employees must also be eligible to participate.

REGULAR CORPORATION

A shareholder-employee of a regular corporation may participate in a Medical Reimbursement Plan without having to report the expense reimbursement as personal income. The corporation deducts the medical expense reimbursement as a business expense (a fringe benefit to employee), without limitation. The Medical Plan must be written and established before the reimbursable medical expenses are incurred. Also, since it may not discriminate

Copyright © 2013 by Small Business Publishing, LLC

between employees, any non-relative employees must also be eligible to participate.

Copyright © 2013 by Small Business Publishing, LLC

TAKING ADVANTAGE OF LOW TAX RATES ON CORPORATE INCOME AND ON DIVIDENDS

GENERAL TAX STRATEGY

Regular corporate income, not paid to a shareholder-employee as salary or bonus, is taxed at the corporation's tax rates. When this income is distributed to the shareholder, it is taxed as a dividend typically at the 15% tax rate (0% if the taxpayer is in the 10% or 15% income tax brackets, and 20% if the taxpayer is in the highest 39.60% tax bracket). The general tax strategy is to minimize taxes by properly setting the shareholder-employee's salary and bonus to "split" income between the corporation and that shareholder-employee, taking advantage of the lowest possible tax rates of each (considering FICA taxes as well). Income tax can also be deferred by delaying the taxable dividend distribution to the shareholder until a future year.

SOLE PROPRIETORSHIP OR DISREGARDED LLC ENTITY

Because a sole proprietorship and a disregarded limited liability company are not considered taxpayers separate from their owner, these entities cannot take advantage of low tax rates on corporate income and dividends.

Copyright © 2013 by Small Business Publishing, LLC

S CORPORATION

Income and/or deductions of an S corporation are generally reported on the income tax return of its owner. The highest corporate tax rate is imposed on any income that, in special circumstances, may be taxed at the corporate level. For these reasons, the S corporation cannot take advantage of low tax rates on corporate income and dividends.

PERSONAL SERVICE CORPORATION

Net income of a personal service corporation (after deducting the shareholder-employee's salary and bonus) is taxable to the corporation at the highest corporate tax rate. Most, if not all, of such a corporation's income is therefore typically paid out each year as salary and bonus to its shareholder-employee. For these reasons, the personal service corporation cannot take advantage of low tax rates on corporate income and dividends.

REGULAR CORPORATION

INCOME TAX RATES
Regular corporations are considered separate taxpayers, subject to graduated federal tax rates (15% on the first $50,000, 25% on the next $25,000, 34% on the next $25,000, 39% on the next $235,000, etc). The corporate net income (that is not paid out to the shareholder-

Copyright © 2013 by Small Business Publishing, LLC

employee as salary or bonus) is generally taxed again at the 15% federal rate when distributed to the shareholder (0% if the shareholder is in the 10% or 15% personal marginal tax bracket).

FICA TAX RATES

The Social Security portion of the FICA tax rate is 12.40% of wages up to the "social security wage base" ($113,700 in 2013). The Medicare portion of the FICA tax rate is 2.90% of all wages, plus an additional .90% on wages in excess of $125,000, $200,000 or $250,000 (depending on filing status). The 12.40% and 2.90% rates are paid 50/50 by the employer and by the employee, with the employer's half deductible for income tax purposes. Since a shareholder in a one-person business is both the employer and the employee, the actual combined FICA tax rate for a corporation in the 15.00% federal income tax bracket would be at least 14.15% on wages up to the "social security wage base" and 2.68% on wages over that base amount. (If the shareholder-employee has wages from other sources equal to the "social security wage base", the actual combined FICA tax rate for a corporation in the 15.00% federal income tax bracket would be at least 7.95% on wages up to the Social Security wage base.)

Copyright © 2013 by Small Business Publishing, LLC

DIVIDENDS PAID

Taxes might be saved if the salary and bonus of a shareholder-employee in the 28.00% federal tax bracket were set, so that the corporation itself reported $50,000 of taxable income, with the $42,500 of after-tax funds paid to the shareholder-employee as a dividend (rather than salary or bonus). In this case, ignoring state income taxes, the corporation would pay $7,500 of income tax (15.00% of $50,000) and the shareholder-employee would pay $6,375 of income tax on the dividend (15.00% x ($50,000 - $7,500)). The total combined federal tax paid by the corporation ($7,500) and the shareholder-employee ($6,375) would be $13,875 (or 27.75% of $50,000).

SALARY OR BONUS PAID

If the $50,000 were paid out by the corporation, via a $46,447 bonus to the shareholder-employee and $3,553 of employer FICA tax (7.65% of $46,447), then the corporation would pay only the $3,553 in FICA tax (no income tax). Assuming the shareholder-employee is not subject to the additional .90% Medicare tax and also has wages from other sources at least equal to the "social security wage base", he/she would then pay $673 in FICA tax (1.45% of $46,447) and $13,005 in income tax (28.00% of $46,447), for a total individual federal tax bill of $13,678. The total combined federal tax paid by the corporation ($3,553) and the shareholder-employee ($13,678) would be $17,231 (or 34.46% of $50,000).

Copyright © 2013 by Small Business Publishing, LLC

TAX SAVINGS

In this example, approximately $3,356 (6.71% of $50,000) might be saved if the salary and bonus of a shareholder-employee were set, so that the corporation itself reported $50,000 of taxable income, with the $42,500 of after-tax funds paid to the shareholder-employee as a dividend (rather than salary or bonus).

If the taxpayer were in a tax bracket higher than 28.00%, subject to the .90% Medicare tax, or did not have wages from other sources equal to the "social security wage base", then the tax savings would be even greater. Also, even if the taxpayer were in the 10% or 15% tax bracket, he/she would still enjoy tax savings by being able to take advantage of a 0% tax rate on dividend income.

Lastly, if the $42,500 dividend were paid to the shareholder in a future year, the $6,375 tax (15.00% of $42,500) would be deferred, and compound interest could be earned each year on this $6,375. (This however assumes no change in the tax rates on dividends in future years.)

Note that the above analysis ignores the impact of state income taxes imposed on both the corporation and individual.

Copyright © 2013 by Small Business Publishing, LLC

TAX STRATEGIES AVAILABLE ONLY TO CORPORATIONS

WITHHOLDING STRATEGY

Penalties are imposed if the owner of a one-person business fails to pay his/her taxes throughout the tax year. Taxes withheld from salary or bonus payments are considered as paid throughout the tax year, regardless of when the salary or bonus is actually paid. There is no penalty imposed if income tax withholding (or evenly paid estimated tax payments) equals or exceeds a "safe harbor" of 100% of the "total tax" reported on the owner's prior year personal tax return (110% if prior year Adjusted Gross Income was over $150,000).

Based on the above rules, the general tax strategy is to withhold from salary and bonus payments of shareholder-employees, income taxes equal to the "safe harbor" percentage of his/her previous year's "total tax" liability. The goal is to avoid the requirement for filing personal estimated tax vouchers, while avoiding penalties for the underpayment of tax throughout the year. By paying taxes through the withholding process, the actual payment of tax can occur very late in the tax year (when the salary or bonus is paid), rather than evenly throughout the tax year (when individual estimated tax payments are required). This improves the cash flow of

Copyright © 2013 by Small Business Publishing, LLC

the business and allows interest to be earned during the tax year on the deferred tax.

A shareholder-employee's optimal salary and bonus is determined each year, depending on the type of corporation, marginal income tax brackets, FICA taxes, and desired retirement plan contributions. If the optimal salary and bonus is not large enough to cover both the employee FICA tax and "safe harbor" withholding, then it may be advisable to make quarterly individual estimated tax payments, rather than increase the salary or bonus (since an increase in salary or bonus may result in additional FICA and income taxes, which might be greater than the penalty that could be avoided).

FISCAL YEAR-END STRATEGY

Corporations are allowed to have a fiscal year-end other than December 31st. Personal service corporations and S corporations typically must make an election under Section 444 of the Internal Revenue Code to have a fiscal year-end (no earlier than September 30th).

A shareholder reports S corporation income on his/her personal income tax return in the calendar year in which the S corporation's fiscal year ends. If the S corporation has a fiscal year-end of September 30, 2013, then the shareholder reports only income from October 1, 2012 through September 30, 2012 on his personal 2013 income

Copyright © 2013 by Small Business Publishing, LLC

tax return. The S corporation must however remit a refundable deposit to the IRS, intended to approximate the income tax on earnings from the end of the fiscal year until December 31st. For example, if an S corporation reported income (before deducting salary and bonus to its shareholder-employee) of $120,000 for the 12 month period ended September 30, 2012, it is "deemed" to have made $30,000 for the three-month period from October 1, 2012 through December 31, 2012. A tax rate equal to 1% above the highest individual tax rate (40.96% in 2013) is applied to the $30,000, less any salary or bonus paid to the shareholder-employee from October 1, 2011 through December 31, 2011, to arrive at the required deposit due May 15, 2013. Each year the refundable deposit is adjusted, using the S corporation's profit (or loss) for the prior tax period.

A fiscal year-end might be beneficial to an S corporation owner in the following situations:

- The business is seasonal and actual income from October 1 through December 31 is more than the calculated "deemed" income (ex/ retailer with a busy Christmas season).
- The business is growing and actual income from October 1 through December 31 is more than the calculated "deemed" income (based on the prior twelve month period, which may have included start-up expenses).
- The shareholder-employee is in a high individual tax bracket and the business is located in a state with no fiscal year-end deposit requirement.

Copyright © 2013 by Small Business Publishing, LLC

In these cases, the required refundable deposit may be less than the combined federal and state income taxes that would be due if the S corporation did not have a fiscal year-end. It may also be beneficial for the S corporation shareholder to know the business income to be reported on his/her personal tax return before December 31st. If the shareholder determines that he/she will be in a higher tax bracket next year, a bonus could be paid from the S corporation immediately before December 31st. The bonus will appear as W-2 income in the current year and will be taxed at the lower current year rate. The bonus reduces the net K-1 income to be reported by the shareholder next year, when he/she is in a higher tax bracket.

It is important to note that a fiscal year-end can be elected only during the beginning months of the S corporation's initial year. Once an S corporation has a December 31 year-end it may not change to a fiscal year-end. An S corporation with a fiscal year-end may however switch to a calendar year-end by having its shareholder pay tax on more than 12 months of income on his/her Form 1040. In this case, the balance of the federal fiscal year-end deposit is refunded (typically after the due date of the Form 1040).

Personal service corporations generally must pay salary and/or bonus to shareholder-employees before December 31st, equal to the income earned from October 1 through

Copyright © 2013 by Small Business Publishing, LLC

December 31st. If this is not done, the corporation may lose some of its deduction for the salary and/or bonus. There is little tax benefit for a personal service corporation to have a fiscal year-end.

Regular corporations may have a fiscal year-end as early as January 31st. In this case, if the bulk of a shareholder-employee's salary and/or bonus could be paid in January with little or no withholding, then the corporation could basically get a tax deduction for salary and/or bonus almost one year before the shareholder-employee would have to report the same as income.

SOCIAL SECURITY BENEFIT STRATEGY

Social security benefits are reduced for recipients age 62 to 65 who have "earned income" above a certain threshold. "Unearned income" however may be received by these individuals without limit and without any reduction of social security benefits. "Unearned income" includes rents, interest and dividends from corporations. Keeping salary and bonus paid to a shareholder-employee at a low, but reasonable, level (while distributing corporate profits via dividends) may preserve social security benefits.

Copyright © 2013 by Small Business Publishing, LLC

EXCLUSION FOR GAIN FROM SMALL BUSINESS STOCK

Individuals who own stock in certain small business corporations for more than five years, may exclude 50% of the gain from the sale of such stock (100% for stock acquired after 9/27/10 and before 1/1/14). Generally, the stock must be newly issued by a regular corporation with at least 80% of its assets used in the active conduct of a qualified trade or business (which excludes professional services, consulting, hospitality, finance, insurance, farming and mining).

FRINGE BENEFIT STRATEGY

Personal service corporations and regular corporations are able to deduct certain fringe benefits without requiring the shareholder-employee, and/or his/her employee-relative, to report such benefits as income. Fringe benefits include accident and health plans (including long-term care insurance), group-term life insurance, dependent care assistance, disability insurance, educational assistance, qualified transportation benefits, retirement advice, contributions to "education savings accounts", cafeteria plans, qualified employee discounts, no additional cost services, working condition fringes, on-premises athletic facilities, and "de minimis" fringes. S corporations, sole proprietorships, and limited liability companies arc able to provide only some of these

Copyright © 2013 by Small Business Publishing, LLC

benefits to its shareholder-employee on a tax-advantaged basis. Each fringe benefit is subject to various qualifications and reporting requirements, the discussion of which is beyond the scope of this book.

Copyright © 2013 by Small Business Publishing, LLC

CONCLUSION

If you are a sole proprietor (or disregarded limited liability company) you may want to form a corporation (or elect to have your limited liability company treated as such). If you are a corporation, you may want to adjust your salary and bonus (and/or your present or future dividends) and related tax withholdings. If you work alone, you may want to hire your spouse, children, or dependent relatives. If you have a SEP, but wish you could make more tax-deductible contributions, you might want to set up a 401(k) Profit Sharing Plan instead. If you and/or your family have significant medical expenses, you might want to establish a Medical Reimbursement Plan.

This booklet is intended to educate and inform you, the one-person business owner. It offers creative and valuable suggestions on how your overall taxes might be reduced. By reading the ideas contained in this book, you will be able to discuss your taxes intelligently with your tax advisor, and determine if he or she is knowledgeable and capable of giving you the proper advice. Only after thorough discussions with a qualified and competent tax professional, should you consider any of the tax-saving

Copyright © 2013 by Small Business Publishing, LLC

ideas presented as being appropriate for you or your business.

With proper tax planning, a significant amount of taxes may be saved each and every year. It is well worth your effort.

Copyright © 2013 by Small Business Publishing, LLC

TAX-SAVING CHECKLIST FOR THE ONE-PERSON BUSINESS

Question	Comment

Registering the Business

If a corporation, or the business has employees:

Have you obtained a "Federal Employer Identification Number" (Form SS-4)? _____

Have you obtained a state tax number? _____

Have you obtained an unemployment tax Number (if different than the state tax number)? _____

Have you received a business license and/or occupancy permit from the county or city in which business is conducted? _____

If the business has more than two employees, has it purchased worker's compensation insurance? _____

If the business is "doing business" in more than one state, has it registered with the other state's tax department and/or secretary of state? _____

Copyright © 2013 by Small Business Publishing, LLC

TAX-SAVING CHECKLIST FOR THE ONE-PERSON BUSINESS

Question	Comment

If a corporation, or if the business
has employees, is owner aware of the
responsibility to collect and/or pay:
- federal corporate income tax?   _____
- federal withholding and FICA taxes?   _____
- federal unemployment tax?   _____
- state corporate income tax?   _____
- state withholding tax?   _____
- state unemployment tax?   _____
- state corporate fee?   _____

Is the business aware of the
responsibility to collect and/or pay:
- state use tax?   _____
- state sales tax?   _____
- county business license tax?   _____
- county personal property tax?   _____
- other tax (ex/ litter, tire, etc)?   _____

Copyright © 2013 by Small Business Publishing, LLC

TAX-SAVING CHECKLIST FOR THE ONE-PERSON BUSINESS

Question	Comment

Deciding whether to be an S Corp (rather than a C Corp)

Is your business eligible to make an
S election:
- a domestic LLC or corp.? _____
- under 100 equity owners? _____
- only one class of stock? _____
- all owners are individuals,
  estates, or qualified trusts? _____
- not a certain type of bank,
  DISC or insurance company? _____

Will your business have no trouble
remaining eligible for S status? _____

Could your business be classified as
a "personal service corporation" and
therefore be unable to take advantage
of the lower corporate tax rates? _____

Does your business expect to
distribute to you, rather than reinvest,
most of its earnings? _____

Is there a good chance that your
business will either be liquidated
or sold in the near future? _____

Copyright © 2013 by Small Business Publishing, LLC

TAX-SAVING CHECKLIST FOR THE ONE-PERSON BUSINESS

Question	Comment

Does your business expect to have
start-up losses which you could use
to reduce your own personal taxes? _____

Are your company's profits, after
deducting a reasonable compensation
to you, expected to exceed
$100,000 to $125,000 per year? _____

Can you be reasonably compensated
at a salary level below the
social security wage base? _____

Will your business benefit from
having a September, October, November,
or December year-end? _____

Do the states, in which your
corporation or LLC does business,
recognize the federal S election? _____

Upon IRS audit, is it possible that business
tax deductions could be disallowed and
reclassified as dividend distributions? _____

Copyright © 2013 by Small Business Publishing, LLC

TAX-SAVING CHECKLIST FOR THE ONE-PERSON BUSINESS

Question	Comment
Are the costs of statutory fringe benefits (ex/ group life, medical & disability plans) provided to you, the owner-employee, insignificant?	_____
Does your business contemplate no (or little) investment in dividend-paying stock of other corporations?	_____
Could the your personal taxes be reduced by issuing stock (thereby shifting income or loss) to your family members?	_____
Do you incur interest expense, relating to your investment in the business, which is not currently deductible (due to your lack of investment income)?	_____
Would your business be unable to utilize the cash method of accounting (ex/ its average revenue exceeds $5 million) if it were not an S corporation?	_____

Copyright © 2013 by Small Business Publishing, LLC

TAX-SAVING CHECKLIST FOR THE ONE-PERSON BUSINESS

Question	Comment

Could your business be subject to the
Personal Holding Company, Accumulated
Earnings, or Alternative Minimum Tax if
it were not an S corporation?   _____

Will your corporation be newly-formed
(or your LLC elect corporate status)
and therefore have no built-in gains or
C corporation attributes or carryovers?   _____

Is your business in a field that would
preclude you from excluding 50% (or 100%)
of the gain from the sale of qualified small
business stock in a regular corporation?   _____

Copyright © 2013 by Small Business Publishing, LLC

TAX-SAVING CHECKLIST FOR THE ONE-PERSON BUSINESS

Question	Comment

Deciding whether to be an LLC (rather than an S Corp)

Is your reasonable compensation equal to, or a bit
less than, the net profit of your business?   _____

Will your business have no benefit from a September,
October, November, or December year-end?   _____

Do the states, in which your corporation or LLC
does business, not recognize S elections?   _____

Would there be no or little personal tax
savings if your business income was
distributed to your family members and
taxed at their marginal tax rates?   _____

Do you incur interest expense, or property
taxes, relating to the business use of your
personal car, which is not currently deductible?   _____

Do you prefer to pay estimated income tax
payments each "quarter", rather than paying
once a year through the withholding process?   _____

Copyright © 2013 by Small Business Publishing, LLC

TAX-SAVING CHECKLIST FOR THE ONE-PERSON BUSINESS

Question	Comment

Does your business employ your children
who are under the age of 18?

If you are receiving early social security
benefits, is your business income less
than the allowable amount above which
such benefits are reduced?

If you have a home office, are you worried
that upon audit the IRS might reclassify your
business occupancy cost reimbursements as
"rent" (jeopardizing their deductibility)?

Does the cost of preparing corporate income
tax returns and payroll tax returns outweigh the
benefits of being taxed as an S corporation?

Does the business have losses or distributions
that are being financed by the business entity's
debt that you have personally guaranteed?

Do you have wages from a job that, when combined
with the net profit of your business, exceeds the social
security wage base ($113,700 in 2013)?

Does your spouse work in your business and does
your family have significant medical expenses not
covered by your current health insurance?

Copyright © 2013 by Small Business Publishing, LLC

TAX-SAVING CHECKLIST FOR THE ONE-PERSON BUSINESS

Question	Comment

Deciding Ownership and Issuing Stock

If an S corporation, might stock be issued to your low-income children (at least 18, or in some cases 24, years of age), or parents, to take advantage of their lower tax bracket? _____

If an S corporation, might interest expense, incurred on debt used to either acquire or carry the stock, be fully deductible on Schedule E of personal return? _____

If a C corporation, might interest expense, you incurred on debt use to either acquire or carry your stock, be deductible (to the extent of investment income) on Form 4952 of your own return? _____

If a corporation, in deciding which assets to contribute in exchange for its stock, has the exclusion of property with either a mortgage over its tax basis or an unrealized loss, been considered? _____

Copyright © 2013 by Small Business Publishing, LLC

TAX-SAVING CHECKLIST FOR THE ONE-PERSON BUSINESS

Question	Comment

If a corporation, would an ordinary deduction (rather than capital loss) be available in the event the corporate stock were sold at a loss or were to become worthless:
- common stock issued by domestic corp? _____
- stock issued in exchange for money or property (other than securities)? _____
- total assets received by the corporation for its stock < $1 million? _____
- less than 50% of corporation's receipts (past 5 yrs) from passive sources? _____
- the loss treated as ordinary is $50,000 ($100,000 if joint) per yr? _____

If an LLC, is either the husband or wife members (but not both), in order to avoid the imposition of self-employment tax on two people (rather than one)? _____

Copyright © 2013 by Small Business Publishing, LLC

TAX-SAVING CHECKLIST FOR THE ONE-PERSON BUSINESS

Question   Comment

Borrowing Funds

If a disregarded LLC or sole proprietor, have you separated debt used for business from other debt (ex/ business credit card, business use portion of car loan, etc), and deducted the interest related to business expenditures on Schedule C?   _____

If an S corporation, have you capitalized the business by borrowing money personally (rather than guaranteeing corporate debt) thus ensuring the current deduction of losses on your personal tax returns?   _____

If a C corporation, have you at least partially capitalized the business by loaning money to your corporation (rather than contributing capital) thus enabling you to receive repayment in the future without tax consequences?   _____

If a corporation, are your loans to/from the corporation properly documented with written notes which, if greater than $10K in aggregate, bear reasonable interest?   _____

Copyright © 2013 by Small Business Publishing, LLC

TAX-SAVING CHECKLIST FOR THE ONE-PERSON BUSINESS

Question	Comment

If a corporation, have you avoided the
necessity to pay non-deductible interest
on funds borrowed from the corporation
to finance your personal expenditures
(unless such borrowings qualify as home
acquisition or equity indebtedness)? _____

Might the business borrow funds from
your children (at least 18, or in some
cases 24, years old) who are in a low
tax bracket so as to reduce your
family's overall income taxes? _____

If an S corporation, are you aware that
you may recognize income when your
loans to the corporation (which have
previously financed corporate losses
deducted on your personal income tax
returns) are repaid? _____

Copyright © 2013 by Small Business Publishing, LLC

TAX-SAVING CHECKLIST FOR THE ONE-PERSON BUSINESS

Question	Comment

Acquiring Furniture & Equipment

Are depreciation write-offs being maximized through the timing of property acquisitions and the careful use of the IRC Section 179 expensing election? _____

Has an inventory of all the property being used by the business been taken (to include assets purchased in prior years for personal use and now used for business) to increase depreciation deductions or decrease property taxes? _____

If a corporation, will the corporation purchase the depreciating assets it will use in its business (rather than having you purchase and lease them to the corporation) to avoid having you incur non-deductible passive activity losses? _____

If a corporation, will you personally purchase the appreciating assets (ex/ real estate) the corporation will use, thus avoiding the recognition of corporate level taxable income when the assets are either distributed to you (S corp) or disposed of (C corp)? _____

Copyright © 2013 by Small Business Publishing, LLC

TAX-SAVING CHECKLIST FOR THE ONE-PERSON BUSINESS

Question	Comment

Has the business adopted a set standard
to differentiate repairs and supplies
(currently deductible) from capital
expenditures (depreciable over time)?   _____

Does the business review its property
acquisitions each year to segregate
"personal property" purchases (rapidly
deducted) from "real property" purchases
(slowly depreciated)?   _____

Has the availability of "bonus depreciation"
been considered to accelerate the deduction
for the purchase of new property (that has
not been expensed under IRC Section 179
mentioned above)?   _____

Copyright © 2013 by Small Business Publishing, LLC

TAX-SAVING CHECKLIST FOR THE ONE-PERSON BUSINESS

Question	Comment

Selecting Accounting Period and Methods

If a PSC or an S corporation, has a Section 444 election (to have a year-end other than December 31st) been considered to possibly defer taxes and improve your personal tax planning? _____

If a C corporation (not a PSC), has a fiscal year been considered so that the personal income taxes on your year-end bonus can be deferred to the next year? _____

Is your business electing to use the accrual method of accounting only when it sells inventory, its payables are expected to rise faster than its receivables, or the cash method is otherwise prohibited by law? _____

If the business is engaged in the performance of long-term contracts, has the completed-contract method of accounting been considered as a possible method to defer income tax? _____

Copyright © 2013 by Small Business Publishing, LLC

TAX-SAVING CHECKLIST FOR THE ONE-PERSON BUSINESS

Question	Comment
If the business is engaged in the sale of inventory, has it considered the simplified LIFO method of accounting to defer tax when inventory levels and costs are rising?	_____
Is the business aware of the interest and overhead capitalization rules for constructed property and inventory?	_____
Has the use of the installment sale method of reporting gain on the disposition of non-dealer property been considered to defer taxes into a lower bracket year and to increase interest earnings for the corporation?	_____
If a C corporation, and part of an affiliated group, has a consolidated income tax return been considered?	_____

Copyright © 2013 by Small Business Publishing, LLC

TAX-SAVING CHECKLIST FOR THE ONE-PERSON BUSINESS

Question	Comment

Compensating Shareholder-Employees

If an S corporation, might overall
payroll taxes be saved by paying you the
lowest reasonable salary and distributing
excess earnings as dividends? _____

If a C corporation, does the corporation
reduce its taxable income (so that
it is taxed at marginal rates lower
than your own) by paying you the proper
amount of compensation and year-end
bonus each year? _____

Have you considered withholding from
your (or your spouse's) salary or year-end
bonus, those income taxes sufficient to
avoid underpayment penalties and/or the
necessity for estimated tax filings? _____

If you are being compensated by two
or more related corporations, have you
considered using a common paymaster to
avoid paying unnecessary payroll taxes? _____

Copyright © 2013 by Small Business Publishing, LLC

TAX-SAVING CHECKLIST FOR THE ONE-PERSON BUSINESS

Question	Comment

If you are under 65 and receiving social security benefits, have you considered incorporating your business, and paying yourself a low but reasonable salary, in order to increase those benefits by avoiding the earned income limitations? _____

If an S corporation, have you considered reducing your salary if it is presently causing an S corporation loss which cannot be deducted on your personal tax return? _____

If a C corporation, would you be able to rebuff an IRS challenge as to the reasonableness of your compensation and thereby avoid having the compensation recast as non-deductible dividends (which would be double taxed)? _____

If a C corporation, is your compensation documented in the corporation's minutes, to make it more difficult for the IRS to reclassify it to a non-deductible dividend distribution? _____

Copyright © 2013 by Small Business Publishing, LLC

TAX-SAVING CHECKLIST FOR THE ONE-PERSON BUSINESS

Question	Comment

Hiring Family and Outside Contractors

Is the business reducing its employment
tax costs by hiring legitimate "independent
contractors" who cannot be considered
disguised "employees" by IRS (Form SS-8)?   _____

Is the business maintaining proper
records for new employees (W-4 & I-9)
and independent contractors (W-9)?   _____

Does the business send 1099-MISC
forms to its non-corporate independent
contractors, lawyers, and landlords who
are paid at least $600 each year for
personal services they perform?   _____

Has the business considered hiring
your spouse on a part-time basis and
paying him/her a low (but reasonable)
wage in order to:
- Cover him/her under the business
  retirement plan (ex/ 401(k)plan)   _____
- Provide other fringe benefits to
  him/her (ex/ "medical expense
  reimbursement plan")   _____

Copyright © 2013 by Small Business Publishing, LLC

TAX-SAVING CHECKLIST FOR THE ONE-PERSON BUSINESS

Question	Comment

- take the child care credit and/or
deduct spousal travel, business
meals, entertainment, and education?   _____

Has the business considered hiring your
children (or parents) who have very little
or no other income and paying them an
amount equal to their standard deduction
(plus perhaps an IRA deduction) in order to:
- Save income taxes (if a corporation)?   _____
- Save income and self-employment taxes
  (if a disregarded LLC or sole proprietor,
  hires a child under the age of 18)?   _____

Have you considered taking your children
(or parents) off the business's payroll
(personally giving them gifts instead) to
save FICA and income tax (when they are
in a higher tax bracket than you?   _____

If your parents have small estates
(well below the exemption) and are in a
low income tax bracket, have you considered
having the corporation pay them wages
which (along with gifts from you) they
could use to purchase a home or other
appreciating asset (which then could be
willed to you tax-free)?   _____

Copyright © 2013 by Small Business Publishing, LLC

TAX-SAVING CHECKLIST FOR THE ONE-PERSON BUSINESS

Question	Comment

Providing Benefits to Employees

If a C corporation, have the following fringe benefit
programs (which can be provided to you and other
employees on a tax-free basis) been considered:
 - group term life insurance (to $50K)?   _____
 - medical expense reimbursement plan?   _____
 - health and hospitalization plans?   _____
 - disability income plans?   _____
 - meals & lodging furnished for the
   convenience of the employer?   _____
 - cafeteria plans?   _____
 - qualified transportation benefits?   _____

If a corporation, does the business
reimburse you for business expenses you
incur on a "dollar for dollar" basis
rather than through an expense allowance)
in order to avoid unnecessary payroll taxes
and to minimize your income taxes?   _____

If an S corporation sponsors a health
insurance plan which covers you and/or
family members, have your premiums been
excluded from social security withholding
(though included in your W-2) and deducted
(to the extent allowable by law) on your
personal income tax returns?   _____

Copyright © 2013 by Small Business Publishing, LLC

TAX-SAVING CHECKLIST FOR THE ONE-PERSON BUSINESS

Question	Comment

If a disregarded LLC or sole proprietor,
has the business considered hiring your spouse
and setting up a "medical expense reimbursement
plan", which reimburses (and deducts) medical
expenses for your spouse and his/her family
(which includes you and your children)?   _____

Have you or the business considered
setting-up a Health Savings Account
program?   _____

If a corporation, has the business
considered contributing to your child's
Education Savings Account, or paying for
retirement planning services?   _____

Copyright © 2013 by Small Business Publishing, LLC

TAX-SAVING CHECKLIST FOR THE ONE-PERSON BUSINESS

Question	Comment

Leasing Assets

Do you analyze whether it is better for the business to lease or buy furniture and equipment by computing after-tax present values under each alternative?

Have personal property leases been reviewed in order to determine whether each is a regular (operating) or capital (finance) lease so that proper tax deductions (ex/ Section 179 expense deduction) can be computed?

Is it possible to shift taxable income to your child (at least 18, or in some cases 24, years of age) who is in a low tax bracket by having the business lease assets from him/her?

If your business has signed an office lease calling for either a period of free rent, or for escalating rents, has the presence of an imputed rent expense deduction been investigated?

Copyright © 2013 by Small Business Publishing, LLC

TAX-SAVING CHECKLIST FOR THE ONE-PERSON BUSINESS

Question	Comment

Have you considered having your corporation construct improvements on land, that it is leasing from you, which will revert to you at the end of the lease term, possibly without tax?   _____

If your business is involved in leasing an automobile, has the "income inclusion" amount been properly reported on the income tax return?   _____

If your business's principal place of business is located in your home, is it possible to take a deduction based on the IRS allowance of $5 per square foot (up to 300 square feet), OR for the business use portion of the actual utilities, repairs, maintenance, and depreciation of the home (based on the square footage used for business) documented by photographs and an occupancy permit)?   _____

If a corporation, can expenses be reimbursed rather than having your corporation "rent" the office space from you?   _____

Copyright © 2013 by Small Business Publishing, LLC

TAX-SAVING CHECKLIST FOR THE ONE-PERSON BUSINESS

Question	Comment

Using a Car for Business

Have you prepared an analysis to determine if it is better for your corporation (rather than you) to own a business vehicle, deduct the related interest, treat the vehicle as if it were used 100% for business, and include an amount of income in your W-2 for the value of your personal usage?

Are vehicle-related deductions being maximized through a comparison of the actual cost method with the standard mileage method, in the year the vehicle is first used for business?

Is written evidence relating to business vs. personal vehicle use being maintained as insurance against an IRS adjustment?

If the standard mileage method to compute vehicle deductions is being used, are the business use portion of car loan interest and personal property taxes also being deducted, and records of the vehicle's basis being maintained?

Copyright © 2013 by Small Business Publishing, LLC

TAX-SAVING CHECKLIST FOR THE ONE-PERSON BUSINESS

Question	Comment

Is the minimum amount of a "luxury" automobile's cost being expensed (under Section 179) so that the current year's maximum write-off is unaffected but the depreciation deductions in the years immediately following the purchase of the automobile are increased? _____

Are you aware that taxable gain and depreciation recapture tax can be avoided by "trading-in" your business vehicle for another business vehicle (like-kind exchange) rather than selling the old vehicle and purchasing a new one? _____

Do you plan the business use of your vehicle to exceed 50%, thus allowing the Section 179 expense and accelerated depreciation deductions? _____

Copyright © 2013 by Small Business Publishing, LLC

TAX-SAVING CHECKLIST FOR THE ONE-PERSON BUSINESS

Question	Comment

Entertaining, Traveling and Giving Gifts

Are you maintaining adequate records for business travel, entertainment and meals (which include date, place, dollar amount, persons present, business relationships and the topic of "substantial business discussions")? _____

Has the business considered having its clients/customers reimburse it for actual meal and entertainment expenditures thus avoiding the 50% reduction by having the reduction passed on to those clients/customers? _____

Are business gifts deducted only up to $25 per donee per year and are records documenting the business relationships of the donees maintained? _____

With respect to out-of-town business travel, are you deducting transportation costs to and from the destination by having "business days" (over four hours spent on business) exceed "pleasure" days? _____

Copyright © 2013 by Small Business Publishing, LLC

TAX-SAVING CHECKLIST FOR THE ONE-PERSON BUSINESS

Question	Comment

Are you deducting the dry cleaning and laundering expenses for clothes soiled while you were away on a business trip (regardless of where the dry cleaning is done)?   _____

Have you considered deducting the standard IRS per diem for travel meals and incidental expenses, rather than actual costs?   _____

Copyright © 2013 by Small Business Publishing, LLC

TAX-SAVING CHECKLIST FOR THE ONE-PERSON BUSINESS

Question	Comment

Distributing Earnings

If a C corporation, are you analyzing
whether to pay out earnings to yourself
in the form of compensation (deductible
by the corporation, but subject to FICA),
or in the form of dividends (which are
non-deductible by the corporation and
therefore taxed twice)?   _____

If an S corporation, have you determined
how best to structure the transfer of
funds to you from the corporation
(dividend distribution, loan, salary,
expense reimbursement)?   _____

If an S corporation, even with relatives as
shareholders, are dividend distributions
paid in proportion to stock ownership
to avoid inadvertently terminating the
S election?   _____

If an S corporation, are dividend
distributions documented in the
corporation's minutes, to make it more
difficult for the IRS to reclassify
them to FICA taxable compensation?   _____

Copyright © 2013 by Small Business Publishing, LLC

TAX-SAVING CHECKLIST FOR THE ONE-PERSON BUSINESS

Question	Comment
If an S corporation, are distributions taken only to the extent of your basis in the corporation (your investment plus your share of cumulative undistributed corporate earnings) in order to avoid a taxable gain?	_____
If an S corporation, have you considered exchanging the debt owed to you by the corporation (the basis of which has been reduced by your share of corporate losses) for additional shares of stock, in order to avoid a taxable loan repayment or distribution, and improve the borrowing power of the corporation?	_____

Copyright © 2013 by Small Business Publishing, LLC

TAX-SAVING CHECKLIST FOR THE ONE-PERSON BUSINESS

Question	Comment

Planning for Retirement

Have you considered setting up a retirement plan in order to defer tax on your share of business earnings and to compensate family-employees on a tax-deferred basis? _____

Have you considered terminating (or merging) an existing Money Purchase Pension Plan, in light of the increased contribution limits for Profit Sharing Plans and Simplified Employee Pensions? _____

Before adopting a Simplified Employee Pension, have the following factors been considered:
- maximum of 25% of compensation can be contributed(up to $51,000)? _____
- no requirement to make contributions? _____
- both full-time employees & part-time workers (who have worked 3 of past 5 years earning around $550/year) must be eligible to participate? _____
- immediate 100% vesting of all contributions is required? _____
- investments selected by employee? _____
- easy & inexpensive administration (no annual government filings)? _____

Copyright © 2013 by Small Business Publishing, LLC

TAX-SAVING CHECKLIST FOR THE ONE-PERSON BUSINESS

Question	Comment

Before adopting a Profit Sharing Plan,
have the following factors been considered:
- maximum of 25% of compensation can
  be contributed (up to $51,000)? _____
- contribution amounts may vary but
  must be recurring and substantial? _____
- only full-time employees over 21
  with 1 year of service (2 years if
  plan calls for immediate vesting)
  must be eligible to participate? _____
- up to 6 years may be required for
  100% vesting? _____
- investments selected by either
  corporate employer or employee? _____
- administration is fairly simple and
  inexpensive (annual 500EZ required
  if > $250,000 in one-person plan)? _____

Before adopting a Defined Benefit Pension
Plan, have the following factors been considered:
- maximum contribution is the amount
  which, when deposited on behalf of an
  employee each year until he/she
  retires, will yield an annual benefit
  of no more than the lesser of his/
  her highest 3 consecutive years of
  compensation, or $205,000 for
  the remainder of the employee's life? _____

Copyright © 2013 by Small Business Publishing, LLC

TAX-SAVING CHECKLIST FOR THE ONE-PERSON BUSINESS

Question	Comment

- contributions are required each year? _____
- only full-time employees over 21 with
  1 year of service (2 years if plan
  calls for immediate vesting) must be
  eligible to participate? _____
- up to 6 years may be required for
  100% vesting? _____
- investments selected by either
  corporate employer or employee? _____
- administration is very complex and
  expensive requiring the use of an
  actuary (annual government filing are
  required each year)? _____

If the business has set up a retirement
plan, has it considered providing
tax-free "qualified retirement planning
services" to you? _____

Before adopting a Savings Incentive
Match Plan for Employees (SIMPLE), have
the following factors been considered:
- maximum contribution (via IRA or
  401(k) CODA) of $12,000 by each
  employee under age 50 ($14,500 by each
  employee over age 50) per year? _____

Copyright © 2013 by Small Business Publishing, LLC

TAX-SAVING CHECKLIST FOR THE ONE-PERSON BUSINESS

Question	Comment

- employer must generally either match employee contributions up to 3% of employee's compensation; or else make a 2% of compensation contribution on behalf of each eligible employee? _____

- employees who received a least $5,000 in compensation from the employer the two previous years, and are expected to receive that amount during the year, are eligible for the plan? _____

- immediate 100% vesting is required? _____

- investments selected by either corporate employer of employee? _____

- administration is fairly simple and inexpensive (annual government filing is required only by trustee)? _____

Before adopting a "one-person" 401(k) Profit Sharing Plan (husband and wife considered "one person") have the following factors been considered:

- the maximum annual contribution of $17,500 by each employee under age 50 ($23,000 by each employee 50 or over)? _____

- the employee elective deferrals are not taken into account in applying the above profit sharing deduction limits to the corporate employee contributions? _____

Copyright © 2013 by Small Business Publishing, LLC

TAX-SAVING CHECKLIST FOR THE ONE-PERSON BUSINESS

Question	Comment
Has the advice of a qualified pension consultant been obtained?	_____

Copyright © 2013 by Small Business Publishing, LLC

HOW JOE's ONE-PERSON BUSINESS SAVES ABOUT $12,000 IN TAXES EACH YEAR

SCENARIO

Joe, age 45, is a consultant who works on his own. He is married and has an 15 year old daughter. Joe's 40 year old wife works part-time as his office manager, but is not paid for her work. His daughter also helps out in the summers without pay. She has no income.

Joe's business is organized as an LLC (treated as a sole proprietorship) with its income and deductions reported on Schedule C of his personal individual tax form 1040. The business grosses $125,000 and nets $90,000 (after paying expenses to vendors). Out of the $90,000, Joe contributes the maximum (about $16,728) to a Simplified Employee Pension plan (SEP-IRA) each year. In Joe's last job, he was paid a salary of $50,000 per year for doing the same basic work he now performs in his own business. Joe and his wife are in the 28% marginal tax bracket. They live in a state without income tax.

The next two pages explain how Joe's one-person business saves about $12,000 in taxes.

Copyright © 2013 by Small Business Publishing, LLC

ELECTING TO BE TAXED AS AN S CORPORATION

Rather than having his business treated as a sole proprietorship, Joe files Form 2553 (Election by a Small Business Corporation), to have the LLC business treated as an S corporation. He has the S corporation LLC pay him a "reasonable" salary of $50,000. As a result, Joe and his business now pays net Social Security and Medicare taxes of about $6,579 (($50,000 x 15.3%)-(28% x ½ x $50,000 x 15.3%)), rather than paying self-employment tax of about $10,936 (($90,000 x 92.35% x 15.3%)-(28% x ½ x $90,000 x 92.35% x 15.3%)). **Joe now saves about $4,357 of self-employment tax each year.**

HIRING DAUGHTER

Rather than having his daughter work in the summer without pay, Joe has the S corporation LLC pay her $3,000 for the summer. As a result, Joe (via the S corporation) and his daughter will incur gross Social Security and Medicare taxes of about $459 ($3,000 x 15.3%), but Joe will save about $904 in income tax (($3,000 x 28%) + (28% x ½ x $3,000 x 15.3%). **Joe now saves about $445 of income tax each year.**

Copyright © 2013 by Small Business Publishing, LLC

SETTING UP A 401(k) PROFIT SHARING PLAN

Rather than contributing only $16,728 to a SEP-IRA, Joe has the S corporation LLC establish a 401(k) plan in which he can make a $17,500 contribution as an "employee" (based on 2013 maximum) as well as the S corporation LLC making a $12,500 contribution as an "employer" (25% x $50,000). As a result, Joe can deduct an additional $13,272 of retirement plan contributions and save about $3,716 in income tax (28% x $13,272).

Rather than having his wife work without pay, Joe has the S corporation LLC pay her $23,333 per year. As a result, Joe (via the S corporation) and his wife will incur net Social Security and Medicare taxes of about $3,070 (($23,333 x 15.3%) – (28% x ½ x $23,333 x 15.3%)), but be able to deduct $23,333 of additional retirement plan contributions. The $23,333, which is comprised of a $17,500 contribution by wife as an "employee" plus a $5,833 contribution by the S corporation LLC (25% x $23,333), immediately saves about $6,533 in income tax (28% x $23,333).

Together Joe and his wife can contribute an additional $36,605 ($13,272 + $23,333) to the retirement plan. Though taxable in the future when distributed from the plan, earnings on retirement plan assets grow tax-deferred, and **the contributions save about $7,179 in current taxes each year** ($3,716 + $6,533 - $3,070).

Copyright © 2013 by Small Business Publishing, LLC

CONCLUSION

By simply –

(1) Electing to be taxed as an S corporation (to avoid self-employment tax),

(2) Hiring his daughter (to shift income to a low tax bracket relative), and

(3) Setting up a 401(k) Profit Sharing Plan and hiring his wife (to defer tax by contributing up to 100% of her salary to a retirement plan)

Joe saves about $11,981 of taxes each year.

How much are you saving?

Copyright © 2013 by Small Business Publishing, LLC

19062885R00045

Made in the USA
Charleston, SC
05 May 2013